# FISHING SKILLS

# Coarse Fishing

## Tony Whieldon

### Introduction by Jim Gibbinson

## WARD LOCK LIMITED · LONDON

© Ward Lock Limited 1984

First published in Great Britain in 1984
by Ward Lock Limited, 8 Clifford Street,
London W1X 1RB, an Egmont Company.

Reprinted 1986, 1988 ,1989

Printed and bound in Italy by
New Interlitho, Milan

**British Library Cataloguing in Publication Data**

Whieldon, Tony
    Coarse fishing.—(Fishing skills)
    1. Fishing—Pictorial works
    I. Title      II. Series
    799.1'2     SH439

    ISBN 0-7063-6280-2

# Contents

**Acknowledgments**
My thanks to Michael, Graham and Bob, whose invaluable
assistance made the marathon a little shorter.

# Introduction

The 1980 National Angling Survey revealed that there are more than three million anglers in Britain, over two million of whom are coarse anglers, making it the largest participant sport in the country.

The same survey also revealed that it is a fast-growing sport which every year attracts a great many newcomers – it is for these would-be anglers that this book has been written.

There is a tendency to think of beginners as youngsters – and while that is usually true, it is not inevitably so. I've known men who held their first fishing rods on reaching retirement age! That is one of the marvellous things about angling – you can enjoy it and be successful whatever your age.

On becoming an angler you gain membership of a special 'brotherhood' (or 'sisterhood', for let us not forget that although it's a male-dominated sport, girls and women can and do become excellent anglers); and the essence of this brotherhood is friendliness. I know of no other sport or pastime in which its participants are so ready to help newcomers.

So how does the aspiring coarse angler make a start? First of all, you must acquire the necessary tackle. In this book you'll find some very sound advice on this particular subject, and I recommend that you pay careful heed to it because ill-chosen tackle will prove to be a serious handicap as well as being a waste of money.

Having obtained your new rod, reel and essential accessories you'll doubtless be anxious to start fishing, which is when you'll realize that you cannot just tackle-up beside your nearest lake or river because virtually every water you'll come across will display 'Private' or 'No Fishing' signs.

Obviously, therefore, it's necessary to know something about the way coarse fishing is organized in this country.

Most waters are controlled by angling clubs which can be joined by paying an annual subscription. Once you become a member you will have unlimited fishing in that club's or society's waters for the whole season. That represents very good value when you consider that the average adult fee will range from £5 to £15 per year; in addition, most clubs offer reduced rates for juniors and pensioners.

You can find out the names and addresses of local club secretaries from your tackle-dealer – alternatively a list may be kept by your nearest public library.

Your tackle-dealer will also be able to tell you if there are any day-ticket waters in your area. These can be fished by anyone who buys the necessary permit. Sometimes the permits have to be obtained beforehand (if such is the case your tackle-dealer will probably sell them), but more usual is the system whereby a water-bailiff collects the money and issues you with your ticket while you are fishing. The cost of day-tickets varies, but 50p to £1 would be about average.

Before fishing either club or day-ticket waters, there is an essential and legal requirement to fulfill – you need to obtain a Water Authority rod licence for your area. These, too, can be bought from your tackle-dealer. An adult's licence will probably cost from £3 to £5, and most authorities have special concessionary rates for juniors.

Make sure you get an annual licence that will cover you for the whole of the coarse fishing season (which in most areas runs from 16 June to 14 March inclusive). Short-term licences are only of use to holidaymakers who don't expect to remain in an area for more than a week or two.

Your coarse fish licence does not, incidentally, enable you to fish for salmon or trout – they are classed as game fish and a different (and more expensive) licence is required.

With your licence and your club-card or day-ticket you are now ready to go fishing. But before you rush eagerly down to your chosen water, I would like to offer you an important piece of advice. Please remember at all times that fish are wild creatures; they are timid and easily frightened, so try to avoid heavy footfalls or sudden movements. Think of yourself as a hunter and think of the fish as a cautious quarry that needs to be stalked, outwitted and tempted.

The non-fishing general public cherish the belief that angling success is largely attributable to luck – when they enquire if you've caught anything, the question is usually phrased, 'Had any luck?'. Experienced anglers know that luck plays little or no part in success – oh yes, anyone can get 'once in a lifetime' lucky and catch

a solitary big fish, or make an isolated good catch – but consistent success is only achieved through skill and knowledge.

By deciding to read about fishing you have taken the first step towards being a successful angler because you've demonstrated that you want to learn. The best way to learn is under the tutelage of an experienced and expert mentor; so those youngsters who learn about the sport from a fishing father or friend are very fortunate – but for those who don't have that advantage the next best way is to read about it.

Many beginners' guides have been written; some have been very good and a few have been excellent, but none have managed to cram so much valuable information between their covers as has this particular volume. It has often been said that a picture can say more than a thousand words – and there's no doubt that angling lends itself particularly well to the pictorial approach, especially when the drawings are of the calibre of those in this book.

Of all the beginners' guides I've seen, this is the one I would most like to have had available when I first took up fishing as a boy.

Jim Gibbinson,
Cuxton, Kent.

January 1984.

# Float rod

Manufactured in fibreglass or carbon fibre — the latter being more expensive but having the advantage of being very light in weight. For the beginner, fibreglass is obviously the practical choice, between 10ft (3.05m.) and 13ft (3.95m) in length. Choose a length to suit your physique.

The complete rod is usually made up of three equal-length sections.

# Rings

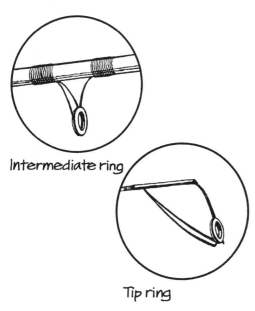

Intermediate ring

Tip ring

Rings are made from chromed steel, stainless steel, aluminium oxide and silicon carbide, which is very expensive, but, being friction free, produces better casting performance as well as prolonging the life span of your line.

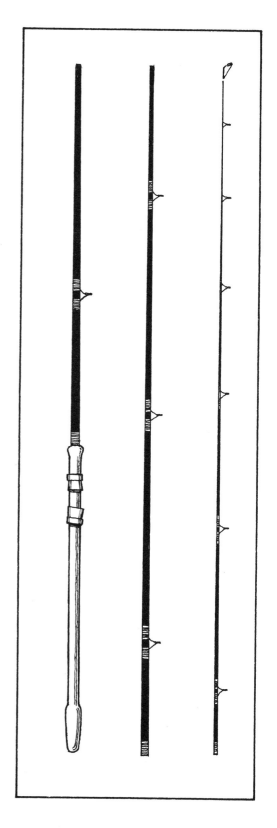

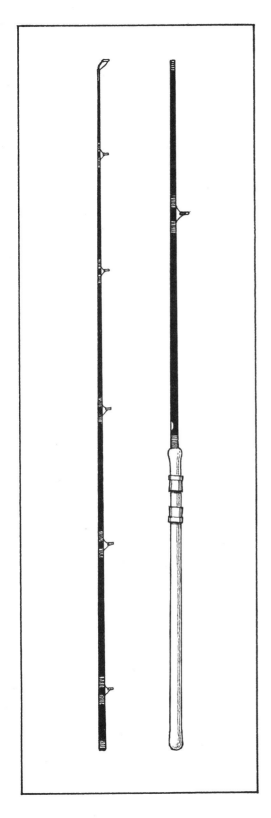

# Leger rod

Ranging in length from 9ft (2·75m) to 11ft (3·35m), leger rods are usually made up of two sections. Some have a special screw fitting built into the tip ring to accommodate a swing-tip or a quivertip. Special quiver-tip rods, with the quivertip built into the rod as a permanent fixture, are also available.

Spigot joint

Reverse glass to glass joint

Swing /quivertip fitting

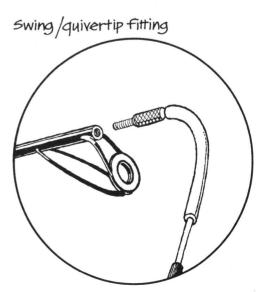

# Fixed-spool reel

By far the most popular reel in use in coarse fishing today. When it is correctly loaded with line the static spool allows extremely long casts to be made. An adjustable slipping clutch mechanism can be set to suit the breaking strain of the line, thus making it virtually impossible for a fish to break the line in snag-free water.

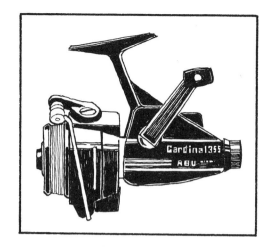

# Centrepin reel

In the hands of an expert this is the ideal tool for trotting a float on fast, strong-flowing rivers like the Trent or the Avon. Very fast recovery of line can be achieved by batting the rim of the drum with the hand.

# Closed face reel

This is a favourite of many top match anglers, superseding the centrepin in its application when trotting a float downstream. Finger-tip control allows fast and efficient fishing.

This reel is also ideally suited to light-line spinning.

# Loading a fixed-spool reel

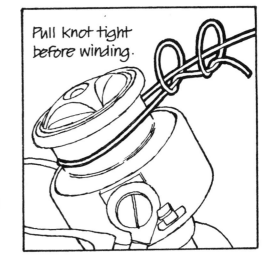

Pull knot tight before winding.

It is most important to load a fixed-spool reel with the correct amount of line. An incorrectly loaded reel will drastically reduce the distance that a small bait should be cast.

Open the bale arm and secure the end of the line to the spool using a double slip knot.

Face the spool towards the reel, and under gentle pressure wind the line on to the reel spool.

The reel is adequately loaded when the line level is about 1mm under the leading rim of the spool.

Have someone holding the line spool and line as you wind the line on to the reel spool.

Fine line spool    Heavy line spool

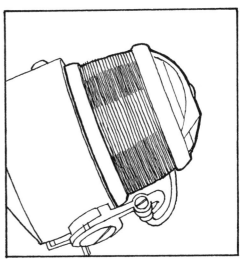

A correctly loaded fixed-spool.

# Hooks

Two types of hooks are used in coarse angling – spade-end and eyed. Eyed hooks can be of the flat variety or down-eyed. Spade-end hooks can be purchased already tied to nylon, but many anglers prefer to tie on their own.

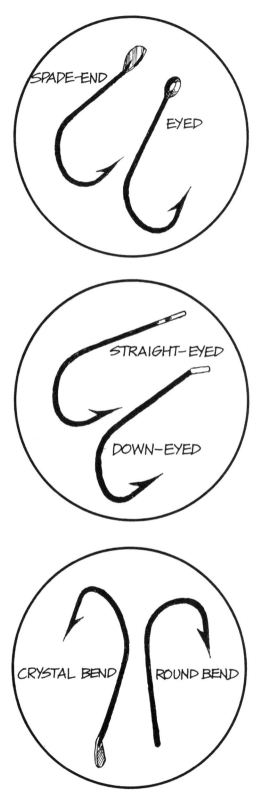

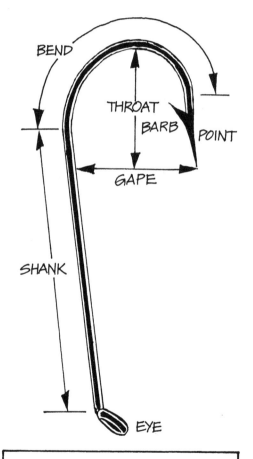

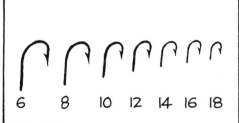

6   8   10   12   14   16   18

# Leads

The Arlesey bomb is, without a doubt, the most popular leger weight. Many anglers use it to the exclusion of all else. A range of Arlesey bombs from ⅛ oz (3g) to 1oz (30g) should meet all your requirements.

The other weights have their uses of course. For example, the drilled bullet is ideal for rolling a bait downstream, whereas the coffin lead has the opposite effect, and anchors the bait.

Barrel leads and jardine spirals are useful for pike fishing, and the ollivette is used with a continental pole.

The plummet is indispensable for finding the depth.

The split shot in its various sizes is a must in every tackle box.

Arlesey bomb

Drilled bullet

Coffin lead

Barrel lead

Jardine spiral lead

Ollivette

Plummet

Split shot

No. 10

No. 8

No. 6

No. 4

No. 1

BB

AAA

SSG

# Floats

Antenna and waggler floats are designed mainly for fishing on stillwaters and very slow—moving rivers.

The antenna float is used at very close range when conditions are perfect with no wind or surface drift.

Straight wagglers, which carry more shot than the antenna, permit longer-range fishing. Some straight wagglers have a very thin cane insert in the tip for greater sensitivity.

Bodied wagglers are for long—range fishing, or where surface movement is a problem.

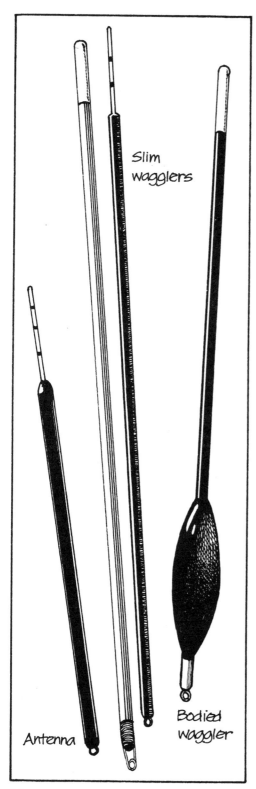

Slim wagglers

Antenna

Bodied waggler

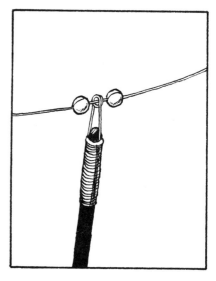

Wagglers are attached to the line by a split shot placed either side of the eye at the base of the float.

Stick, Avon and balsa floats are all intended for fishing on running water.

The stick float is used, with best results, not too far out from the rod tip and trotted down—stream. This slender float is ideal for roach, dace and chub.

The Avon, being more buoyant in the top area, can cope with a wider range of conditions than the stick. The ideal float for the beginner to learn the art of trotting the stream.

The balsa is the big brother of fast-water floats. In its larger sizes it is ideal for fishing big baits, like luncheon meat or worms, in deep, fast swims.

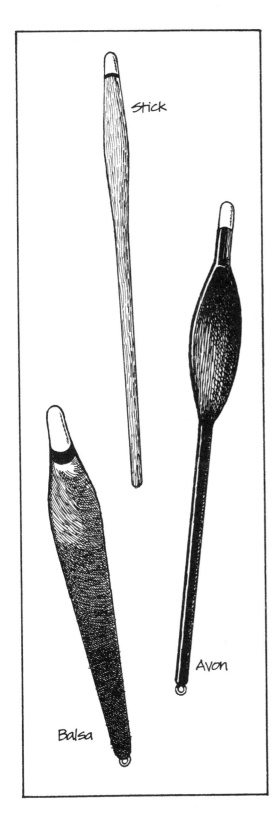

Stick

Avon

Balsa

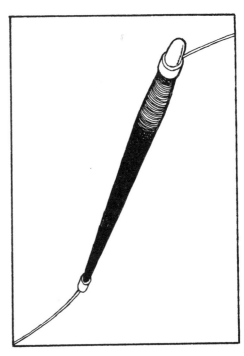

Sticks, Avons and balsas are all attached to the line top and bottom.

# Finding the depth

If you intend to present your bait on, or very close to the bottom, the most accurate and positive way to achieve this is with the aid of a plummet.

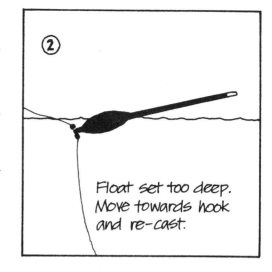

Float set too deep. Move towards hook and re-cast.

### ①

Estimate the depth and fix the float in position.
Hook a plummet to the end of the line by passing the hook through the eye at the top and inserting it into the cork at the base. Then cast to the area you intend to fish.

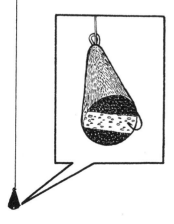

Float set too shallow. Move away from hook and re-cast.

④   Just right.

# Sinking the line

Whenever a waggler is being used the line must always be submerged between the rod tip and the float.

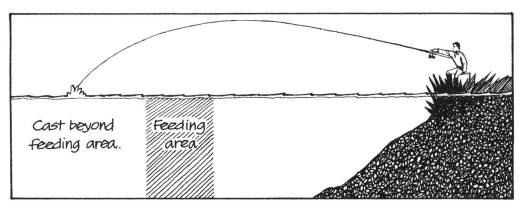

Cast beyond feeding area.

Feeding area

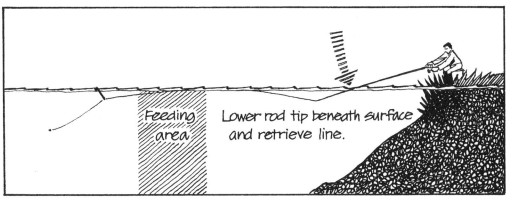

Feeding area

Lower rod tip beneath surface and retrieve line.

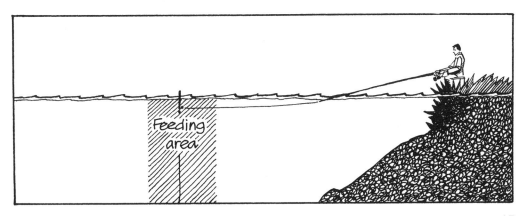

Feeding area

# Shotting patterns

# Stillwater

Each type of float is made in a variety of sizes; therefore it would be confusing to quote specific sizes in shot.

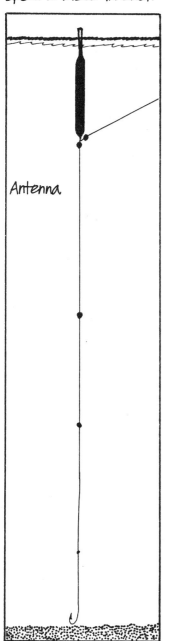

Antenna

Straight waggler

Bodied waggler

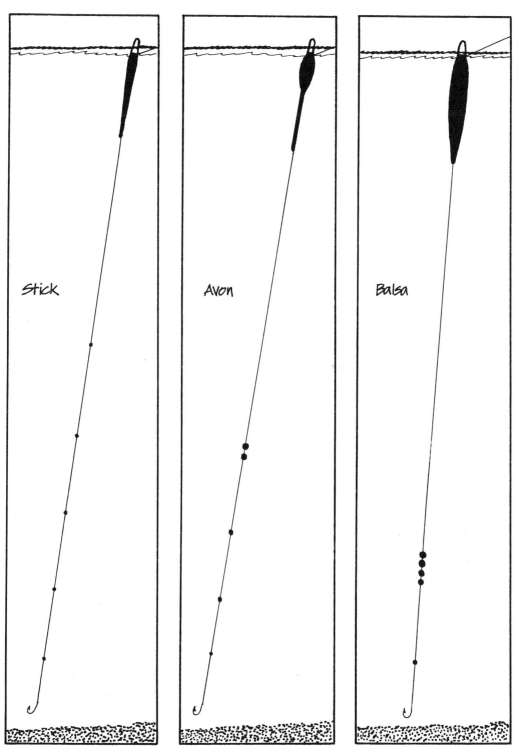

Stick

Avon

Balsa

# Leger terminal rigs

Free line: This very basic rig is used with large baits. It offers no resistance to a taking fish and is especially suited to carp fishing.

Running leger with Arlesey bomb: With the added weight this rig is capable of fishing baits both large and small at long range. A split shot or leger stop is used to hold the lead in the required position.

Running leger with drilled bullet: Ideal for trundling a bait downstream.

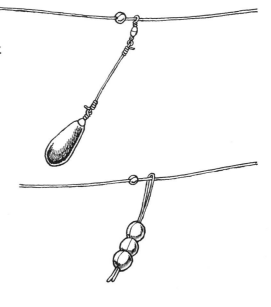

Running link leger with Arlesey bomb: This rig enables the fish to take more line before it comes up against the resistance of the bomb, and in the process gives an early bite register at the rod.

A very light link leger can be made by squeezing two or three swan shot on to the nylon link.

# Leger terminal rigs

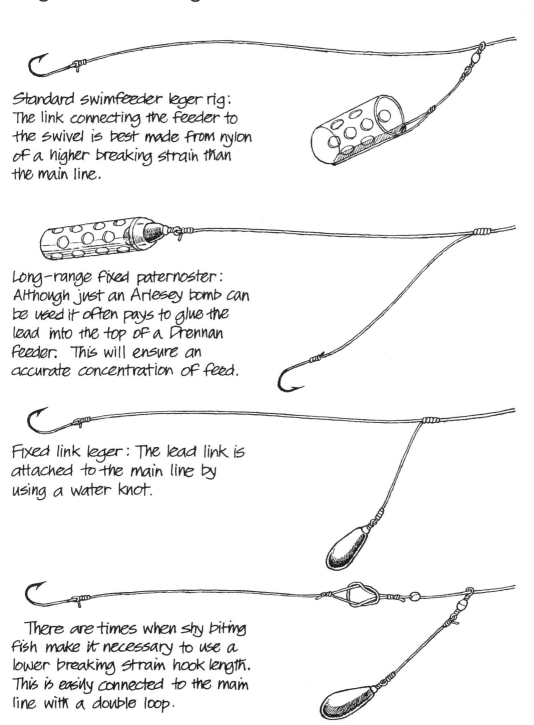

Standard swimfeeder leger rig:
The link connecting the feeder to
the swivel is best made from nylon
of a higher breaking strain than
the main line.

Long-range fixed paternoster:
Although just an Arlesey bomb can
be used it often pays to glue the
lead into the top of a Drennan
feeder. This will ensure an
accurate concentration of feed.

Fixed link leger: The lead link is
attached to the main line by
using a water knot.

There are times when shy biting
fish make it necessary to use a
lower breaking strain hook length.
This is easily connected to the main
line with a double loop.

# Swimfeeders

A swimfeeder enables the angler to present the feed and the bait in the same area.

Concentration of the fish shoal will therefore increase the likelihood of the hook-bait being given some attention by the feeding fish.

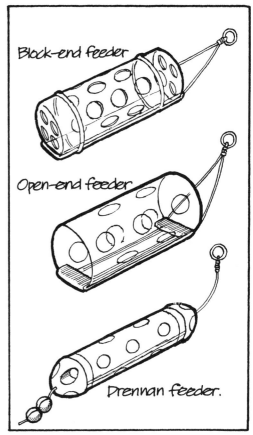

Block-end feeder

Open-end feeder

Drennan feeder.

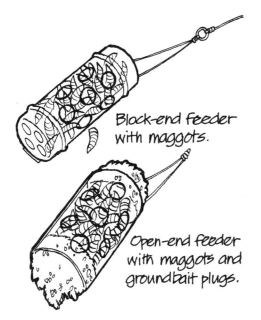

Block-end feeder with maggots.

Open-end feeder with maggots and groundbait plugs.

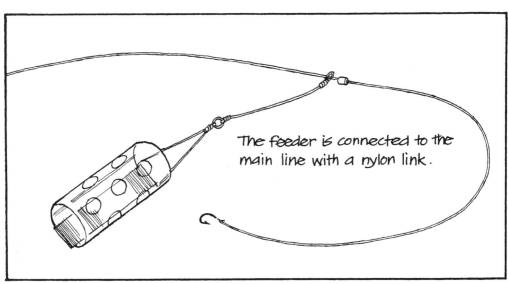

The feeder is connected to the main line with a nylon link.

# Overhead cast

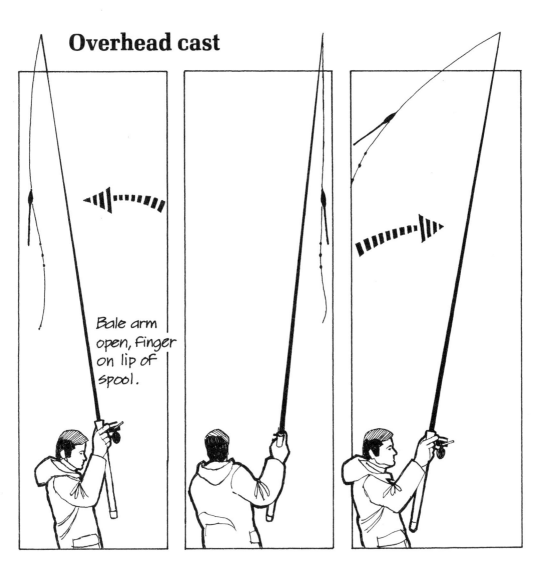

Bale arm open, finger on lip of spool.

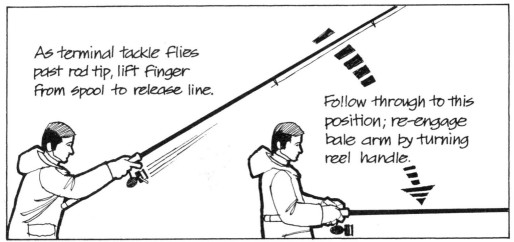

As terminal tackle flies past rod tip, lift finger from spool to release line.

Follow through to this position; re-engage bale arm by turning reel handle.

# Underarm cast

This cast is most useful when fishing in a confined space, where overhanging foliage makes it impossible to use the overhead cast.

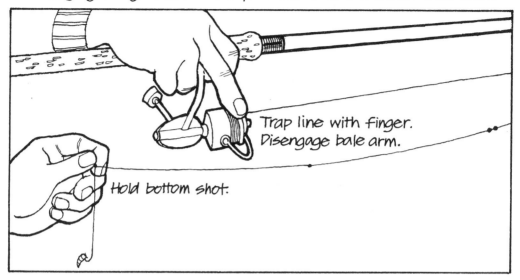

Trap line with finger.
Disengage bale arm.

Hold bottom shot.

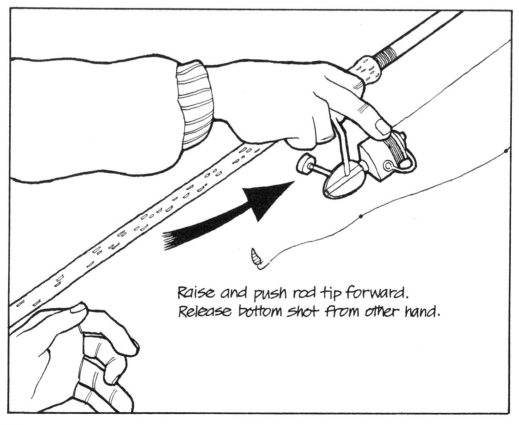

Raise and push rod tip forward.
Release bottom shot from other hand.

# Underarm cast

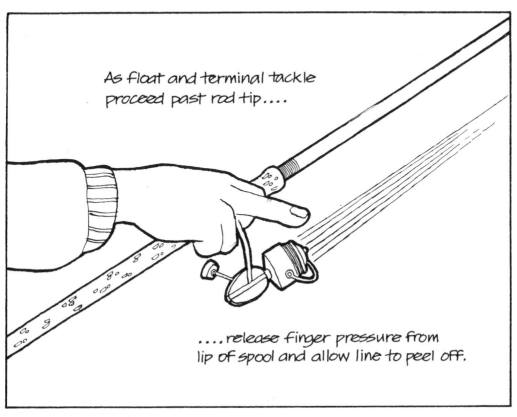

As float and terminal tackle proceed past rod tip....

....release finger pressure from lip of spool and allow line to peel off.

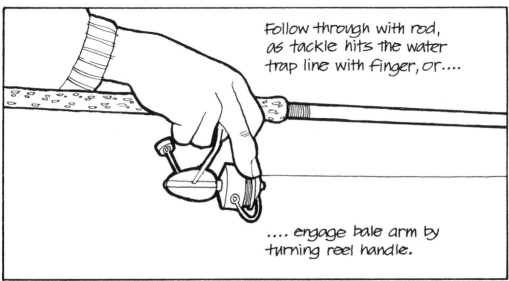

Follow through with rod, as tackle hits the water trap line with finger, or....

.... engage bale arm by turning reel handle.

# Species

ROACH: A very common fish found in most lowland lakes and rivers. The eye is quite red, with tinges of red on the lower fins. The general body colour is silver, but on older, larger specimens it might be rather brassy.

RUDD: A deeper bodied fish than the roach. The eye is gold and the pelvic, anal and tail fins are bright red. The pelvic fins are positioned forward of the dorsal fin.

DACE: More streamlined than the roach, this little fish likes running water, but is also found in some lakes. The eye is yellowish, and the edge of the anal fin is concave.

CHUB: The anal fin is convex— a sure means of identification when compared with a dace. They like running water, especially where trees overhang the river. They are also found in some lakes.

PERCH: Found in lowland lakes, ponds and rivers. It is a handsome fish with a row of spines along the dorsal fin, and some on the gill covers. The body is generally green. The pelvic and anal fins are vivid red.

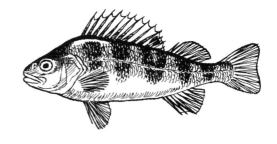

BRONZE BREAM: Very slow moving rivers, lakes and canals are the haunts of this fish, which is never happier than when rooting around in mud. Its protractile mouth enables it to suck in small organisms from the soft bottom.

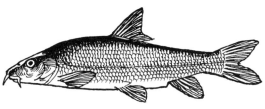

BARBEL: A powerful fish found in clear, fast-running water. Favoured haunts are weir-pools, depressions in the river-bed and beneath under-cut banks.

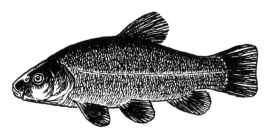

TENCH: Found in very slow rivers and lakes, where it feeds on the bottom. Quite often though it will show itself on the surface. Colour is predominantly olive, and the eye is small and red.

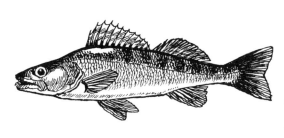

ZANDER: A fierce predator which prefers to hunt its prey in open water. The younger fish hunt in shoals, but as they grow larger a more solitary existence is adopted. Like the pike this fish is armed with a set of sharp fangs. It prefers still or very sluggish, murky water.

PIKE: Another fierce predator, but having a preference for weed beds where it lies in wait for its prey, which is just about any species of fish. It will not hesitate to attack a member of its own species.

CARP: A dweller of lakes, ponds and slow rivers. Three varieties of cultivated carp exist, namely the COMMON, MIRROR and LEATHER. If left to breed in a wild state, the offspring will revert to the original slim shape of the WILD CARP.

# Species

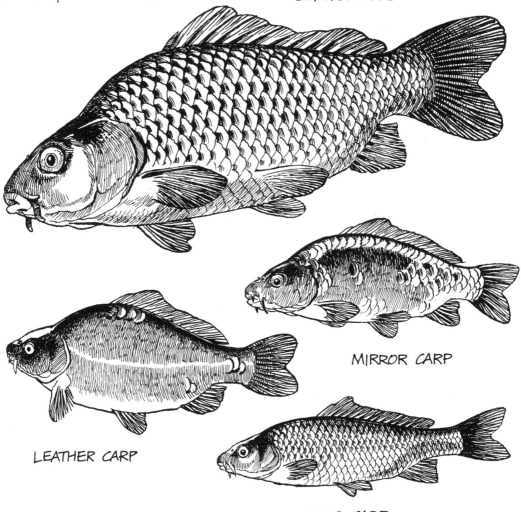

COMMON CARP

MIRROR CARP

LEATHER CARP

WILD CARP

   The habits of these varieties of carp are identical, and the same fishing tactics can be employed for all of them. The wild carp does not grow to such a large size as the common, leather or mirror varieties, but what it lacks in size is more than compensated for in speed.

CRUCIAN CARP: This hardy species never grows to any great size, but will often thrive in waters where other species cannot. It lacks barbels, and feeds mainly on the bottom.

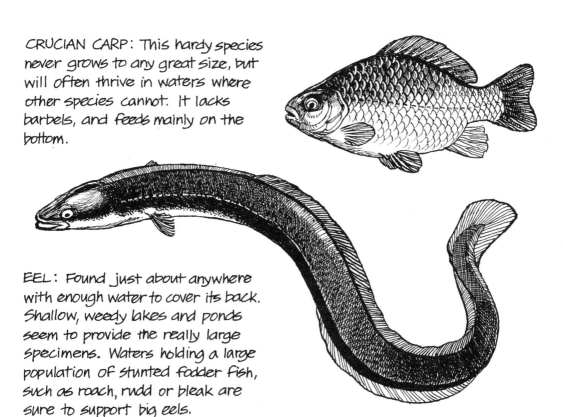

EEL: Found just about anywhere with enough water to cover its back. Shallow, weedy lakes and ponds seem to provide the really large specimens. Waters holding a large population of stunted fodder fish, such as roach, rudd or bleak are sure to support big eels.

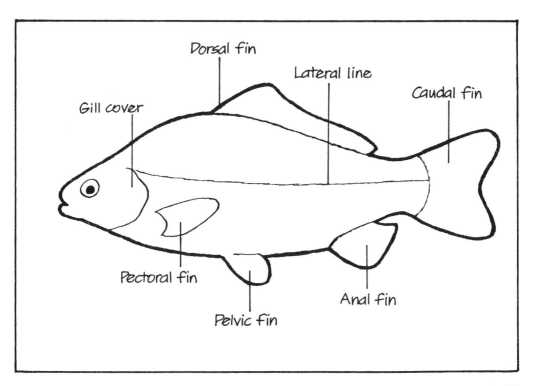

Dorsal fin

Lateral line

Caudal fin

Gill cover

Pectoral fin

Pelvic fin

Anal fin

# Baits

MAGGOT: Without a doubt the most widely-used bait for coarse fish. More than one type of maggot can be bought commercially. The main one is the larvae of the blow fly, and is used mainly as a hook bait. Pinkies and squatts are smaller and are used as feeder maggots. Another type is the gozzer, which is an excellent bait for bream. To keep maggots at their best store them in a cool place.

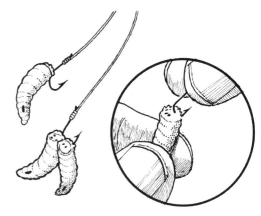

To hook a maggot, squeeze gently between finger and thumb. Nick the hook into the flap of frilly skin.

CASTER: The next stage of metamorphosis before the maggot becomes an adult fly. They are ideal as loose feed and are often mixed with groundbait. If used as a hook bait they are very likely to produce better quality fish.

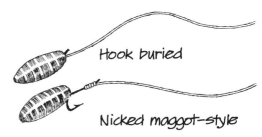

Hook buried

Nicked maggot-style

How to bury a hook in a caster.

WASP GRUB: An excellent bait for chub, and many other species. To acquire them is no easy matter. Your local pest control expert may be able to supply you with a couple of nests complete with grubs.

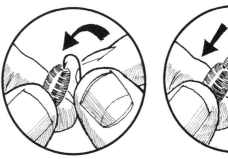

LOBWORM: Definitely a big fish bait. Walk out on to a lawn on a warm night, with a torch, and if the ground is moist you will see them lying full length on the grass with just the tips of their tails in their holes. If you are stealthy, you can fill a bait container in a very short time. They are best kept in damp moss or newspaper.

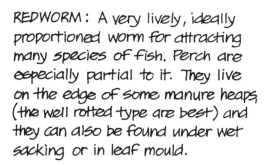

REDWORM: A very lively, ideally proportioned worm for attracting many species of fish. Perch are especially partial to it. They live on the edge of some manure heaps, (the well rotted type are best) and they can also be found under wet sacking or in leaf mould.

BRANDLING: Another very lively worm found in manure heaps. Fish take them readily enough, but they are rather unpleasant to use as they exude a pungent yellow liquid, when the hook is inserted. Unless you have no other choice they are best left in the manure heap. Mount them on the hook as you would a redworm.

BREAD FLAKE: Fresh bread is best suited for this. Simply pinch out a piece of bread from the middle portion of the loaf. Squeeze part of it on to the rear end of the hook shank, but leave the bread which covers the bend of the hook in its natural state.

BREAD CRUST: A very versatile bait. It can be used floating on the surface, resting on a sub-merged weedbed, or floating just off the bottom. A bait favoured by many big fish hunters.

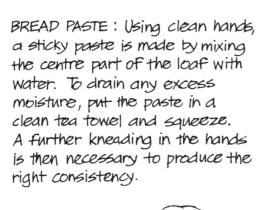

BREAD PASTE: Using clean hands, a sticky paste is made by mixing the centre part of the loaf with water. To drain any excess moisture, put the paste in a clean tea towel and squeeze. A further kneading in the hands is then necessary to produce the right consistency.

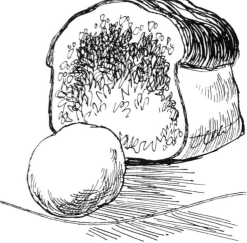

LUNCHEON MEAT: An excellent bait for barbel and chub.

CHEESE: This is one of the old favourites; some anglers use nothing else. The wide variety gives plenty of scope for experiment. As cheese tends to harden after being submerged in water it is best to test the consistency, to ensure that the hook will penetrate through the bait when the strike is made.

POTATO: Used almost exclusively for carp, although if mashed and converted to paste form will interest many other species. New potatoes are the best type, and need to be boiled, but not to the extent where they start to crumble; remember, they have to stay on the hook during the stress of casting.

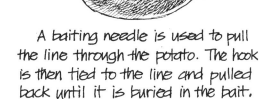

A baiting needle is used to pull the line through the potato. The hook is then tied to the line and pulled back until it is buried in the bait.

SWEETCORN: An excellent bait for carp and tench. Constantly buying the pre-cooked tinned variety can be expensive if it is used for loose feed as well as hook bait. However, by purchasing loose maize from your local corn merchant you can use this as loose feed, and by using the larger, tinned kernels on the hook the cost over the season will be considerably reduced.

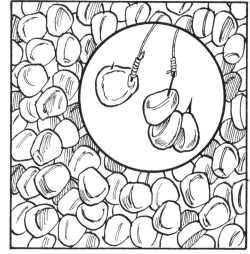

HEMPSEED: On a water which is fished regularly with hemp, this is a deadly bait from the word go. On waters where its use is infrequent or unknown, it may take a while for the fish to become accustomed to it, but thereafter will have a devastating effect. Before use, it has to be soaked for twenty-four hours, or simmered for about forty-five minutes, until it splits.

ELDERBERRY: Another very seasonal bait that will tempt roach, dace and occasionally bigger fish like chub and barbel. Loose feed three or four berries with every cast. Split shot should not be used in conjunction with hempseed or elderberry. Instead use a twist of lead wire.

# Groundbait

This is a mixture that is introduced into the swim you intend to fish, or are fishing. It can be introduced at regular intervals prior to the actual fishing day, (known as 'pre-baiting'). Tench respond to this treatment particularly well. Brown breadcrumb with water is a good base for groundbait.

When mixed with water it should have a consistency which allows it to be fashioned into golfball-sized balls, without crumbling. Samples of hookbait can be integrated with the base, eg., maggots or casters.

These balls are introduced by hand, or with the aid of a catapult, to the swim, where they disintegrate. The introduction of more groundbait during the fishing session is sometimes necessary. Heavy groundbaiting can often do more harm than good. Little and often is a more sensible and productive policy.

# Loose feed

Introduced into the swim during the process of fishing. The particles are usually, but not always, the same as the hook-bait.

Fish such as roach, rudd, dace and chub, will often rise towards the surface to intercept sinking feed particles, and in cases like this, fishing a slow-sinking bait works best (fishing on the drop).

Bottom-feeding fish such as tench, bream and carp, will be more likely to approach the loose feed as it lies on the bottom.

# Bite indicators for legering

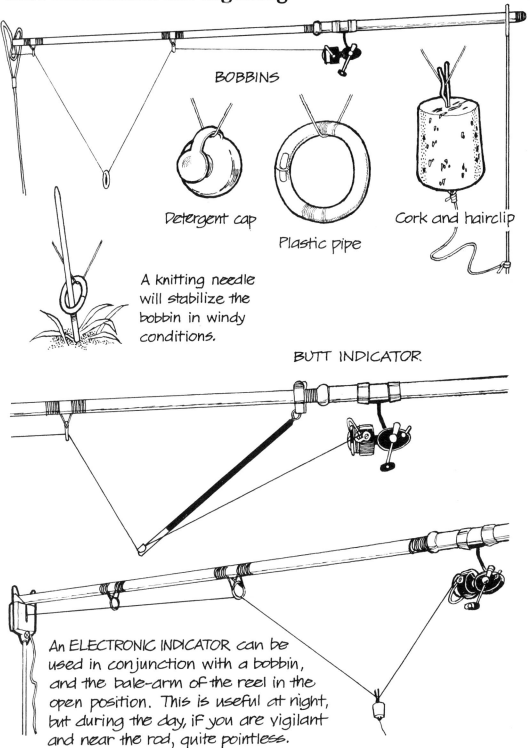

BOBBINS

Detergent cap

Plastic pipe

Cork and hairclip

A knitting needle will stabilize the bobbin in windy conditions.

BUTT INDICATOR

An ELECTRONIC INDICATOR can be used in conjunction with a bobbin, and the bale-arm of the reel in the open position. This is useful at night, but during the day, if you are vigilant and near the rod, quite pointless.

# Fishing with a swingtip

Cast out and let the terminal tackle sink to the bottom. Place the rod on the rests and tighten the line with a few turns of the reel handle. When the swingtip is hanging off the vertical by about 25° it is in the correct fishing position.

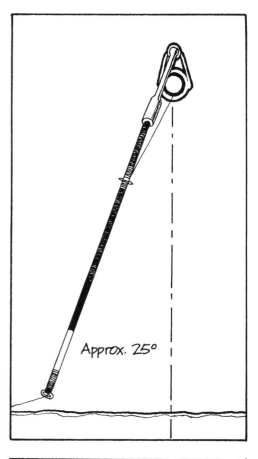

Approx. 25°

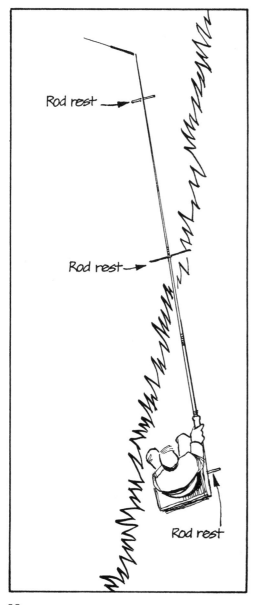

Rod rest

Rod rest

Rod rest

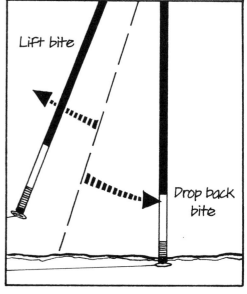

Lift bite

Drop back bite

# Fishing with a quivertip

The quivertip has an advantage over the swingtip in as much as it can be used on running water as well as stillwater. For normal conditions, position the rod rests and rod as you would for a swingtip. After casting, tighten up to the lead so that the tip adopts a slight curve. This will enable the tip to straighten up when a drop-back bite occurs.

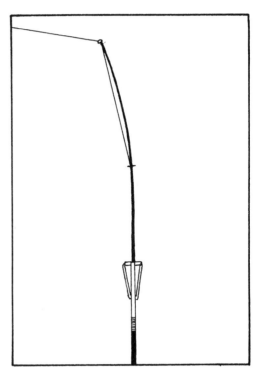

Attitude of quivertip after the line has been tightened – ready for a bite.

If you are fishing the far bank on a river and the current is strong in mid-stream, you can overcome the problem of water pressure affecting the sensitivity of the tip by propping up the rod. This will lift a lot of line clear of the water.

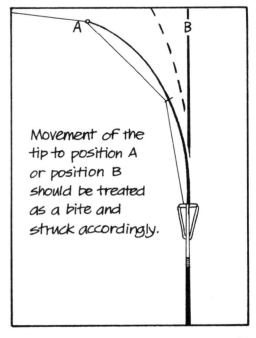

Movement of the tip to position A or position B should be treated as a bite and struck accordingly.

# Trotting the stream

Suspend a bait beneath a stick, Avon or balsa float, let the current carry the end tackle in a natural fashion through the swim, and at the same time allow the pull of the current to take line from the spool of the reel. In the past, the centre-pin reel was used for this style of fishing, but nowadays the closed-face and fixed-spool reels are used more often than their predecessor.

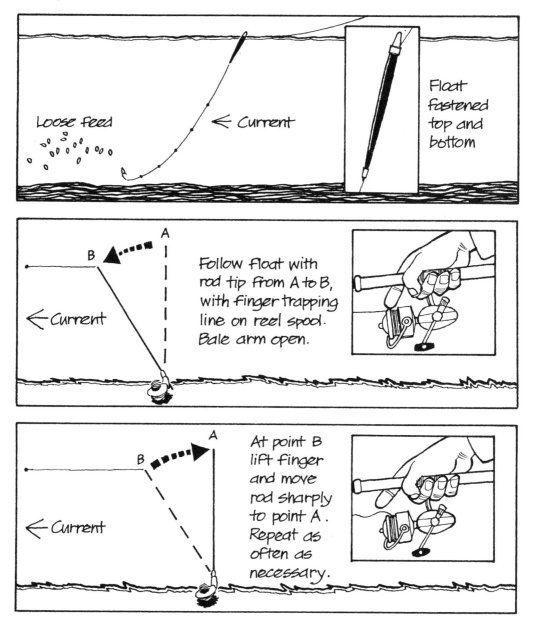

Loose feed

← Current

Float fastened top and bottom

A

B

← Current

Follow float with rod tip from A to B, with finger trapping line on reel spool. Bale arm open.

A

B

← Current

At point B lift finger and move rod sharply to point A. Repeat as often as necessary.

# Mending the line

Trotting the stream directly downstream from the rod tip is fairly straightforward, but the problem of a bow in the line presents itself if the bait is being fished well out from the rod tip. If the bow is ignored the pressure of the current will build up within the bow and pull the float and bait across the stream in a most unnatural manner. Mending the line will cure this in its early stages.

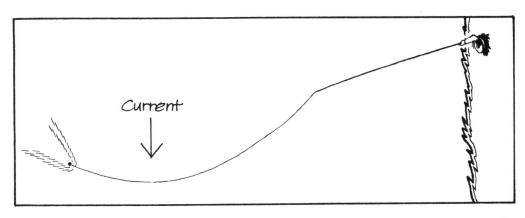

Current

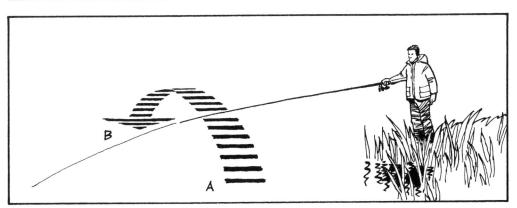

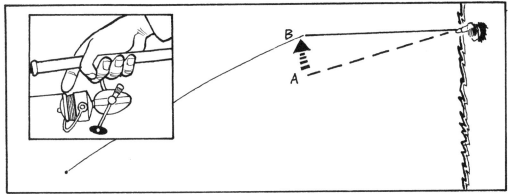

# Laying on

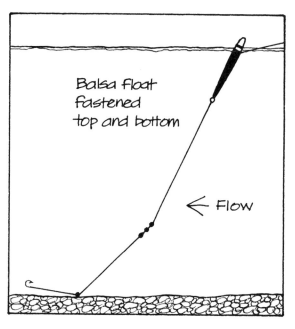

Balsa float
fastened
top and bottom

← Flow

This method is employed on running-waters. It comes into its own during winter, when the river is usually running higher, with a bit of colour. It is best to fish directly down-stream from the rod tip. Set the float over-depth. After casting, place the rod in a rest, and tighten-up until the float adopts the attitude shown in the diagram.

# The lift method

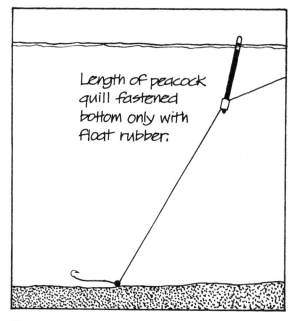

Length of peacock
quill fastened
bottom only with
float rubber.

A stillwater method, ideally suited to tench. The float is set over-depth and a large single shot is pinched on the line just above the hook. As with the above method, the rod must be placed in a rest until a bite occurs.

A typical lift-bite is signalled by the float lying flat on the surface, but occasionally it just slides out of sight.

# Slider float

Used when the depth being fished is greater than the length of the rod, or when bankside foliage restricts overarm casting. For fishing still-waters a large-bodied waggler is employed as a slider, while on running water a special balsa float with two rings is used.

In order to stop the float at the required distance above the bait, a sliding stop knot is tied onto the main line.

## SLIDING STOP KNOT

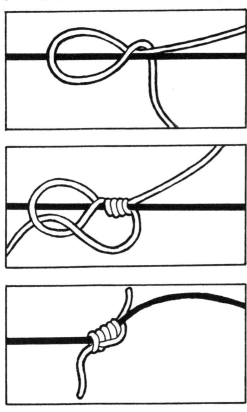

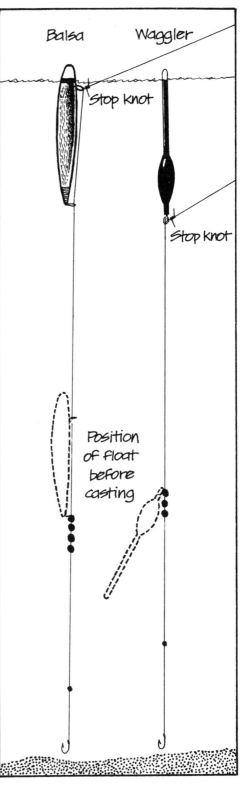

# Methods for catching                    Roach

It is probably true to say that more anglers fish intentionally for roach than for any other species of fresh-water fish. Roach will accept a wide variety of baits. Bread (paste, flake and crust), maggot, caster, hemp, redworm, cheese and lobworm tail have all accounted for this fish.

Choice of hook-size will of course depend on the size of bait being used at the time. Stillwater roach can be found close to weed beds, where a bait presented on the bottom will be best to start with.

Maggot, caster, hemp, bread paste: Hook, size 16 or 18.

Bunch of maggots, redworm: size 14.

Lobworm tail, bread flake or crust: size 12 or 10.

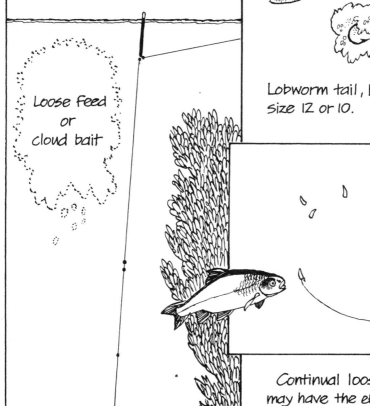

Loose feed or cloud bait

Continual loose-feeding, however, may have the effect of drawing the fish up, whereupon 'fishing on the drop' tactics can be employed.

Running-water roach should be looked for in eddies and slacker areas of water out of the main current.

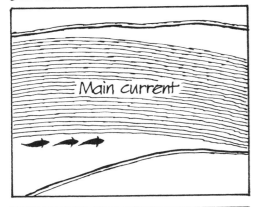

Main current

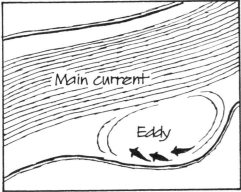

Main current

Eddy

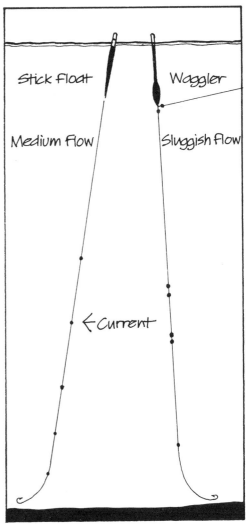

Stick float

Waggler

Medium flow

Sluggish flow

←Current

Running-water float tackle

Light leger tackle and a quiver-tip will produce roach, especially if the water is clearing after a flood.

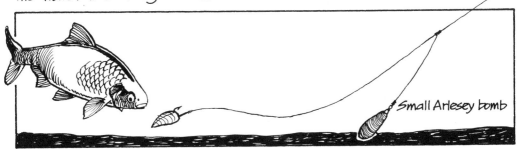

Small Arlesey bomb

# Rudd

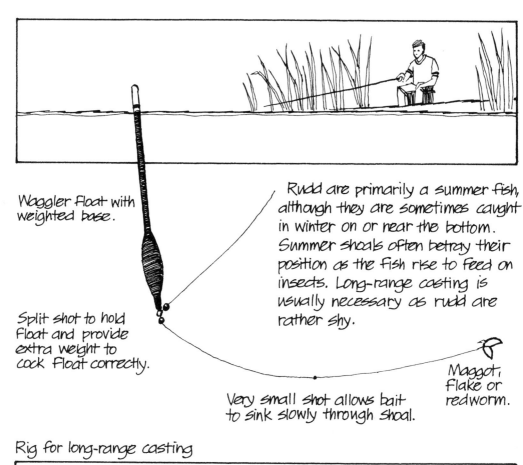

Waggler float with weighted base.

Rudd are primarily a summer fish, although they are sometimes caught in winter on or near the bottom. Summer shoals often betray their position as the fish rise to feed on insects. Long-range casting is usually necessary as rudd are rather shy.

Split shot to hold float and provide extra weight to cock float correctly.

Maggot, flake or redworm.

Very small shot allows bait to sink slowly through shoal.

Rig for long-range casting

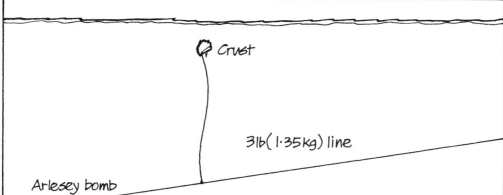

Crust

3lb (1·35kg) line

Arlesey bomb

# Dace

Dace form large shoals and can be found widely distributed over most rivers, sometimes accompanied by small chub. Their presence is often displayed by dimples on the surface as they rise to take insects.

A bait suspended beneath a stick float and preceded by loose-feed will usually attract these fast biters.

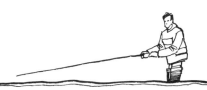

They can also be taken on light leger tackle and a quivertip. This tackle is best employed in slack areas of water near the bank, or where a shallow runs into deeper water.

Two swan shot link leger

Dace found in these quieter areas of water tend to be a better stamp of fish, and will often bite more boldly, taking larger baits such as bread flake or redworm.

# Chub

Small chub are gregarious, and can form large shoals. Without knowing what to look for it is easy to confuse a small chub with a large dace. The key to positive identification lies in the anal fin.

Trotting the stream with a stick or Avon float is a good way of getting to grips with these smaller chub.

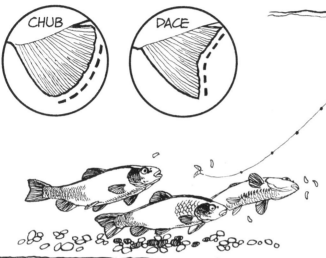

A legered bait fished in conjunction with a quiver tip, and presented fairly close in will bring good results, especially in the winter when the river is running high.

Large chub are more solitary, and very shy. They like to have a roof over their heads. Overhanging trees, rafts of driftwood, overhanging banks, are all likely chub spots. Just let a leger roll into these sorts of places. If there is no response after a while, then move on to another chubby-looking hole. Here are just a few chub baits: maggots, casters, bread, cheese, luncheon meat, wasp grubs, crayfish, slugs and worms.

# Chub

A large, bushy artificial fly cast under, or close to overhanging bushes, will often account for large chub.

Chub living in very small streams are often visible, and wary, therefore the angler should proceed with extreme caution. It is best to fish freelined baits, presenting the offering just behind the fish. It does not matter if the bait makes a splash as it hits the water, for this usually results in the fish making a quick turn, and grabbing the bait confidently.

Some huge chub exist in certain stillwaters. Illustrated below is the unconventional tackle used for the capture of a 7lb (3.00 kg) specimen from an Oxfordshire gravel pit.

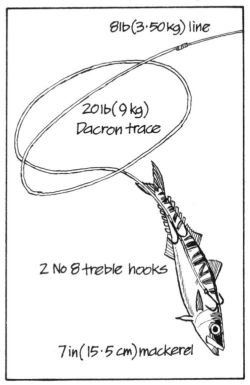

8lb (3.50 kg) line

20lb (9 kg) Dacron trace

2 No 8 treble hooks

7in (15.5 cm) mackerel

# Perch

Small to medium-sized perch are very rapacious, and can be caught on the most basic of tackle. They congregate close to weed beds, piles, sunken tree limbs and roots, etc.

A redworm is probably the best bait for these smaller predators.

Perch will readily take a small spinner or spoon. A leger rod can be used for this form of fishing.

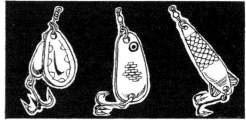

A selection of perch lures.

Large perch lead a more solitary existence, preferring to lurk in the deeper areas of lakes. Long-distance casting is often required to reach the perch holes, therefore the use of a leger rig will be necessary.

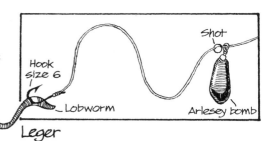

Hook size 6

Lobworm

Shot

Arlesey bomb

Leger

Running paternoster

The best time to fish for large stillwater perch is during the winter months. At this time of the year natural food is scarce and hook-baits are taken readily. Locating these deep water predators is not so easy, as they tend to concentrate in small areas in the deepest parts of the lake. Here is a simple and effective procedure for finding the likely 'hot-spots' where the really big perch lie during winter.

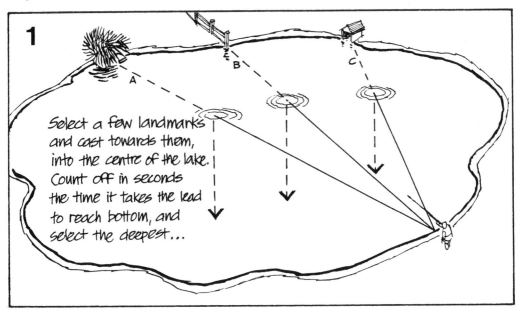

**1**

Select a few landmarks and cast towards them, into the centre of the lake. Count off in seconds the time it takes the lead to reach bottom, and select the deepest...

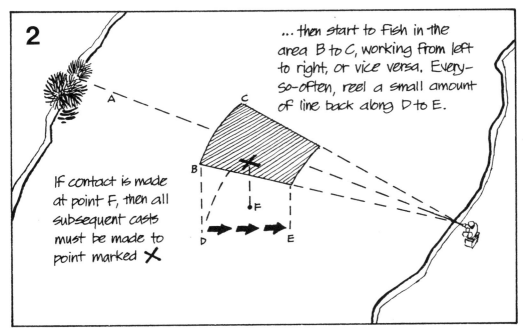

**2**

... then start to fish in the area B to C, working from left to right, or vice versa. Every-so-often, reel a small amount of line back along D to E.

If contact is made at point F, then all subsequent casts must be made to point marked ✗

# Bream

Bream tend to shoal and feed in depressions on the river or lake bed. Where shallower water starts to drop away into deeper water is always a good place to present your bait.

Introduce some balls of groundbait into the swim prior to fishing.

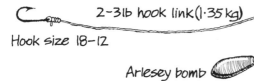

2-3lb hook link (1·35 kg)

Hook size 18-12

Arlesey bomb

3-4lb main line (1·80 kg)

Terminal leger tackle

False bite

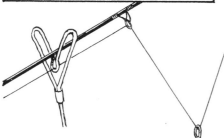

False bites are all too common when the bait is lying in a dense shoal of bream, and some of them look very convincing on the bite indicator. The solution is to have the bobbin suspended well down from the rod and to resist the temptation to strike until it has risen all the way.
Baits: Maggots, Bread flake, Redworms.

# Tench

This, more than any other, is a fish of summer. A dawn session, prior to a hot day, will usually bring the best results. Tench will, however, continue to feed right through the day if it is overcast and mild.

It is good policy to groundbait your swim daily, prior to fishing.

If weedgrowth is very prolific, a rake pulled through the swim will clear most of it and will also disturb the bottom, which in turn will attract fish into the area.

Leger terminal tackle can be the same as that used for bream.

Length of peacock quill

Large bait eg., bread flake or bread paste

BB shot

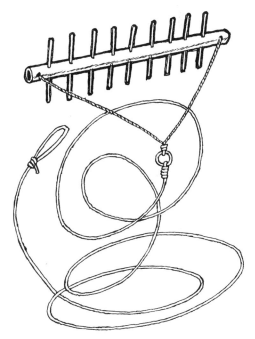

Baits: Bread flake, paste and crust, lobworm, redworm, sweetcorn, maggot, caster.

The tench float rig will also serve very well for catching bream.

# Barbel

Like the carp, this is another fish that requires a special type of rod. The combination of a powerful fish and its environment (fast-flowing water) will necessitate using a rod with a through action.

The rod should be about 11ft (3·35m) in length.

An Avon float will cope with the smaller baits and medium-depth swims, but a balsa will be required for large baits and deep swims with a heavy flow.

Baits: Maggot, hempseed, worms, sausage, luncheon meat, cheese.

A rolling leger is the ideal method with which to search deep holes and weirpools, favourite barbel haunts. Use just enough lead to keep the tackle down, but not enough to hold bottom.

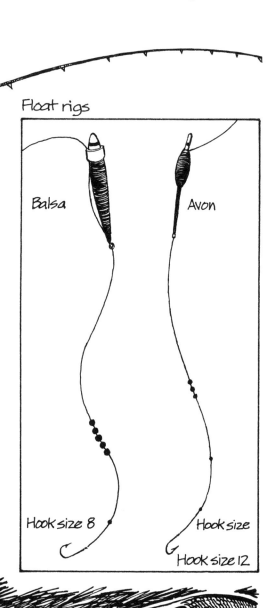

Float rigs

Balsa

Avon

Hook size 8

Hook size

Hook size 12

# Eel

Eels, especially small ones, can be a nuisance when they gorge a bait intended for other fish. Medium to large specimens, however, when specifically pursued, can provide a unique and exciting form of fishing.

A carp rod will be necessary for hauling this powerful fish away from underwater snags.

Legering at night, or during the day if the weather is humid and overcast, will produce the best results.

Terminal tackle

Swivel

12 in (30 cm) Wire trace

10 lb (4.50 kg) main line

Small Arlesey bomb for casting a worm

Link swivel

Wire trace

Split shot prevents bait from sliding up the trace.

Hook size 2

Dead roach, rudd, bleak or dace, 4 in (10 cm) in length.

Lobworms

There is usually no need for any additional weight when using a dead fish bait. It will be necessary, however, to puncture the bladder of the dead fish, so that it sinks.

Thread the trace through the bait with a baiting needle.

# Pike

For the occasional pike session a carp rod will suffice, for casting small dead-baits, and spinning; but for regular use something a bit heavier will be needed. A stepped-up carp rod with a test curve of 2½ lb (1·10 kg) will be far more suitable.

Probably the most sporting and most enjoyable way of taking pike is by fishing a plug, or a lure.

Here is a small selection of the many patterns obtainable today.

Light-line plug fishing is usually practised with a short bait-casting rod, coupled with a multiplier or an Abumatic reel.

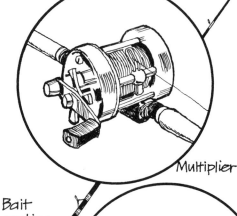

Multiplier

Bait casting rod

Abumatic

## Lures

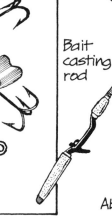

Abu Toby

Abu Atom

Mepps

## Plugs

When using lures that spin, it is advisable to attach an anti-kink device, or lead, to the line, in order to prevent line twist.

Wye lead

Fold-over lead

'Anti-kink' ball bearing swivel

Some plugs sink slowly under their own weight; others float on the surface when stationary, but dive and wobble when retrieved. Their action is very typical of a small wounded fish, and irresistible to a hungry pike.

# Pike

Fishing with a static deadbait is likely to produce the really large specimens. To start with, you will need a collection of wire traces, and it is best if you make your own.

Swivel

18in (45cm) cable-laid wire approx. 20lb (9kg) test.

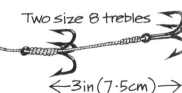

Two size 8 trebles

←—3in (7·5cm)—→

Bait: Roach, rudd, bleak, trout, mackerel, herring, sprat.

How to mount a legered deadbait.

A legered deadbait can also be fished in conjunction with a float.

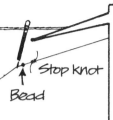

Stop knot

Bead

Swan shot

Balsa pike float

57

# Zander

The tackle employed for catching pike can also be used for zander, except perhaps the hooks, which should be a size smaller.

When legering for zander (and pike), it is a good policy to leave the bale arm of the reel in the open position; this enables the fish to run freely with the bait. Whilst waiting for a bite the line can be kept taught by wedging it beneath a line clip.. A run will pull the line free.

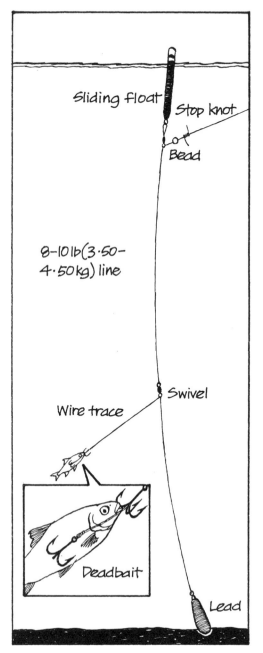

Sliding float

Stop knot

Bead

8-10lb (3·50-4·50kg) line

Swivel

Wire trace

Deadbait

Lead

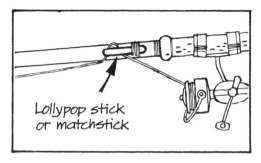

Lollypop stick or matchstick

Zander will readily attack a spinner or a plug. It is generally more productive to fish in open water, well clear of weedbeds.

# Crucian carp

This sporting little fish which never grows to any great size 3lb (1·35kg) is about average), can be taken on similar tackle to that used for roach.

If surface drift becomes a problem, fasten the float bottom only, and/or use a slightly larger float and split shot.

Cloud groundbait as for roach.

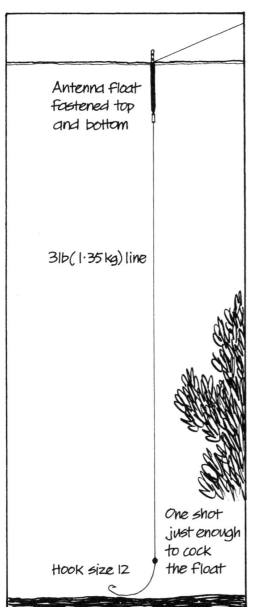

Antenna float fastened top and bottom

3lb (1·35 kg) line

One shot just enough to cock the float

Hook size 12

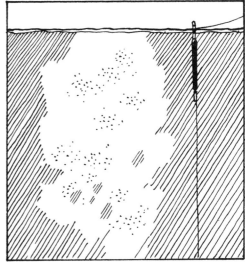

Baits

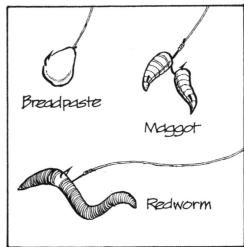

Breadpaste

Maggot

Redworm

# Carp

The carp is a very powerful fish, requiring an equally powerful rod to cope with his fury, when hooked.

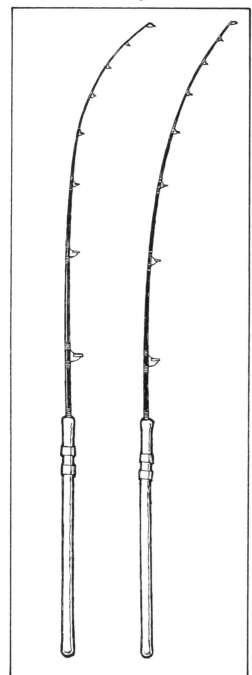

Floating bread crust

When carp are visible on the surface, this is the best method to use. A sandwich loaf makes the best floating crusts.

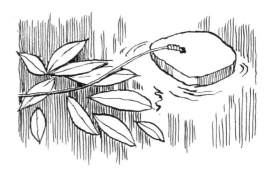

A gap in or alongside a weedbed is a good position for a crust.

When a carp takes the crust, don't panic and strike prematurely — wait until the line begins to run out across the surface of the water.

# Carp

Anchored crust

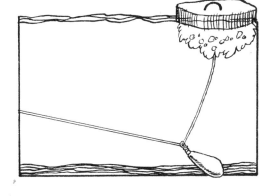

Suspended crust

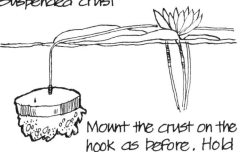

Mount the crust on the hook as before. Hold the crust under water and squeeze out the air.

At night, carp patrol the margins and can be tempted with a crust fished in this manner. The indicator is a length of silver foil.

Leger tackle should be kept as basic as possible.

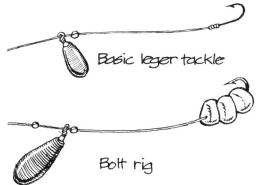

Basic leger tackle

Bolt rig

Finicky carp can be difficult to hook. When a bolt rig is used, the fish panics when it feels the hook, and makes a positive run.

More good carp baits

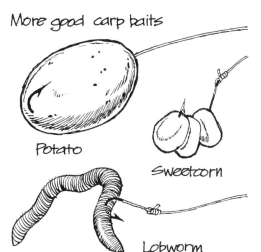

Potato

Sweetcorn

Lobworm

61

# How to play and land a fish

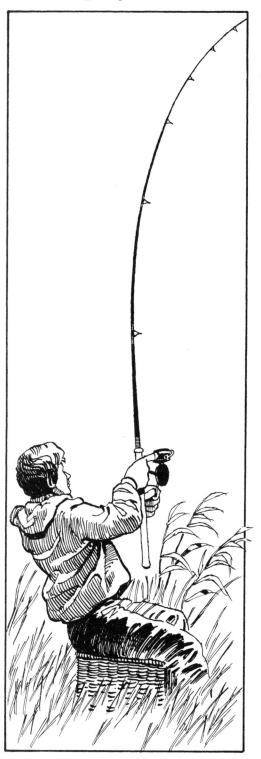

On hooking a fish, especially a large one, keep the rod tip well up and maintain a steady pressure. Never point the rod at the fish. The slipping clutch on the reel must be adjusted prior to fishing so that it yields line when the pressure on it is just below the breaking strain of the line.

If a hooked fish makes a dash for an area where underwater snags exist, it can be turned by applying side-strain.

Have the net close at hand. When the fish shows signs of tiring, slip the net into the water and keep it stationary. Never jab at the fish in an attempt to scoop it out. Bring the fish to the net, not the net to the fish.

# Handling and hook removal

Always wet your hands before handling a fish. Grip the fish firmly but gently just behind the gill openings. If the hook is lightly embedded near the front of the mouth, it is possible to remove the hook with your finger-tips, otherwise use a disgorger.

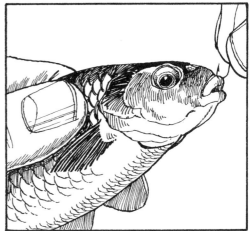

With larger fish, it is best to leave the fish lying in the damp net while you remove the hook. Artery forceps are best. When they are locked a really good grip is maintained on the hook, which can be gently eased out. A damp towel positioned between the hand and the fish is advisable, as large fish like carp are very strong and need some holding if they suddenly decide to leap about.

In the case of pike, it is advisable to wedge open the mouth with a lump of cork, or a gag, before attempting to remove the hooks. If a gag is used, cover the sharp ends with cloth or cork to avoid damaging the jaws of the fish.

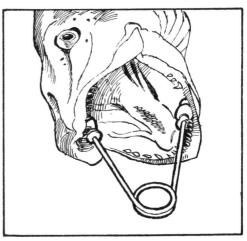

# Weighing a fish

The first requirement for this procedure is a knotless mesh bag or sling. This is saturated with water to prevent removal of protective slime from the fish. Place the sling on a soft base of grass or moss and gently slide the fish inside, first making sure that your hands are also wet. At a pinch, a landing net can be used (with the handle removed of course). Don't forget to allow for the weight of the landing net frame.

Never weigh a live fish in this manner; it will damage the delicate gill filaments.

Fish weighed in this manner will lie quietly until the whole procedure is over.

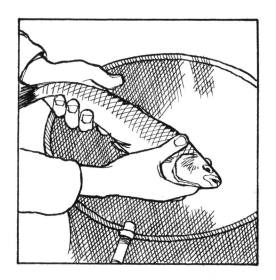

# Retaining and returning fish

Fish should only be retained in a knotless keepnet, which is well covered by water, preferably in a shaded area. Never keep them for any length of time; in fact there is no point in retaining them at all unless they are to be weighed or photographed at the end of the fishing session.

Larger fish like carp, tench and pike are best retained in keepsacks where they lie quietly.

Never throw a fish into a net, but gently place it inside using wet hands.

When returning fish, gently gather up the net until the area occupied by the fish is reached; place the mouth of the net underwater and allow the fish to swim off.

A large fish should be held with both hands underwater in an upright position until it swims away.

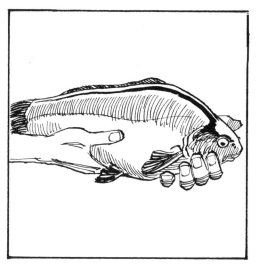

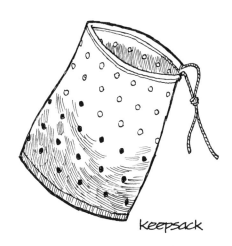

keepsack

# Accessories

## Keepnet

This item should always be as large as you can afford. Never buy one less than 6ft 6in (200 cm). 13ft (400 cm) would not be too big if a good swim was located holding large fish. A long net is also more practical where the water is shallow near the bank.

All keepnets have a screw fitting to accommodate a bank stick. To stop the net collapsing in the water, it is a good policy to secure the bottom of the net with another bank stick.

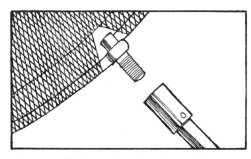

Screw fitting for bank stick.

Bank stick retaining bottom of net.

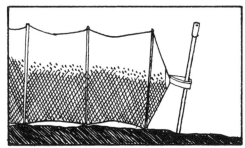

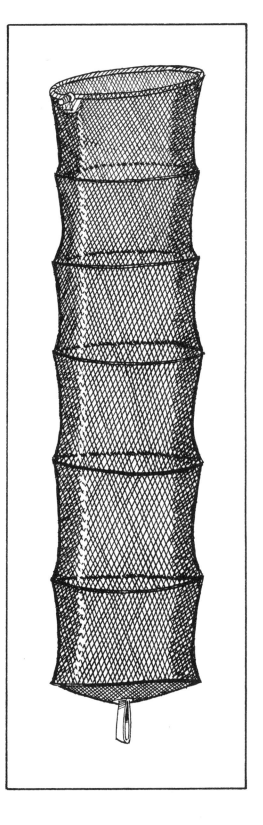

# Landing net

The two basic shapes for landing net frames are circular and triangular. Materials used include alloy and fibreglass, both of which are used to make the handles. The same mesh is used for both keepnets and landing nets. This is a knotless nylon mesh, which does not harm the fish.

Frame sizes vary from the average-sized match net about 24in (60cm) to the specimen hunter's model of 36in (90cm)

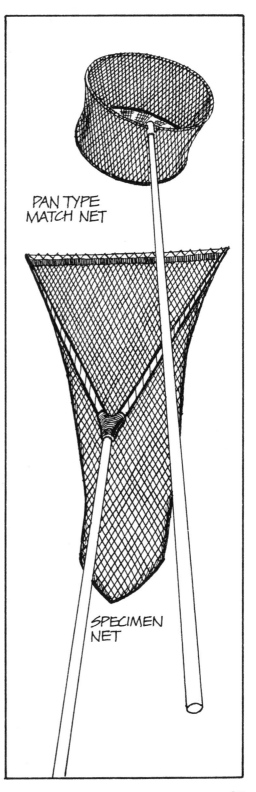

PAN TYPE MATCH NET

SPECIMEN NET

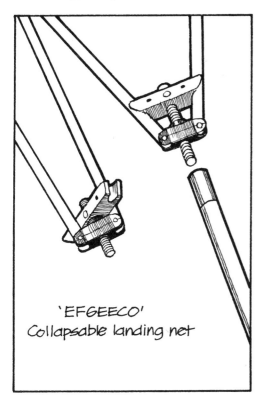

'EFGEECO'
Collapsable landing net

# Baskets, boxes and seats

Although being superseded by more sophisticated material, the cane basket is still popular.

The Fibreglass models are so well manufactured that they can actually be placed in several inches of water to provide a seat.

Metal-framed box-seats like the 'Efgeeco' model are excellent.

Where a lower profile is necessary, usually when carp fishing, a low, folding chair is ideal.

Traditional cane basket

Fibreglass tackle container

'Efgeeco' Tubular framed tackle carrier

# Catapult

If loose feed or groundbait balls have to be delivered at medium or long range a catapult is essential. It is advisable to have a spare length of elastic available in case of breakage.

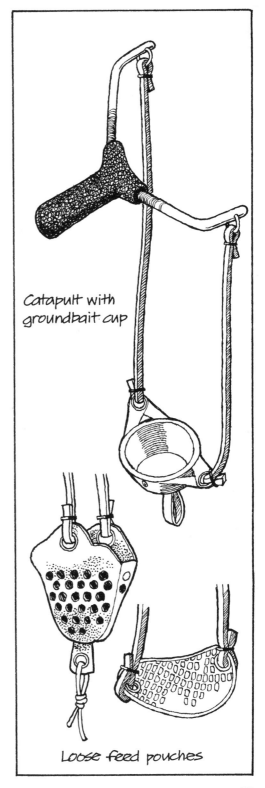

Catapult with groundbait cup

Loose feed pouches

If the catapult is fired with the handle in a vertical position, a painful rap on the knuckles will be experienced. To fire, tilt the handle over to one side.

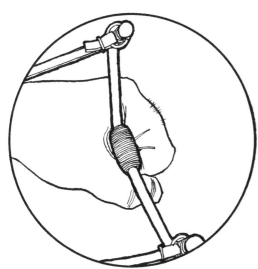

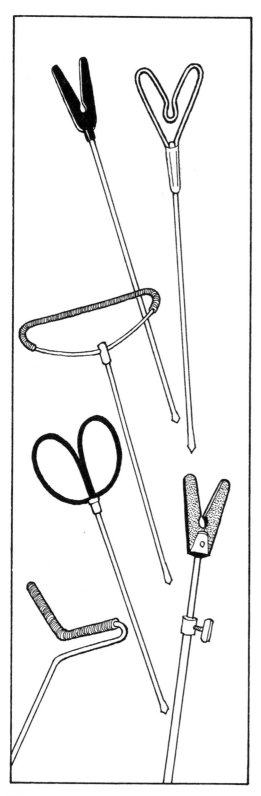

# Rod-rests and bank sticks

Rod-rests come in a large variety of shapes and sizes but with one basic purpose, to support the rod while the angler waits for a bite. Many rests have an opening in the top to prevent the line being trapped by the rod; thus allowing line to be taken by a running fish after it has taken a legered bait.

Bank stick with screw fitting for taking detachable rod-rest.

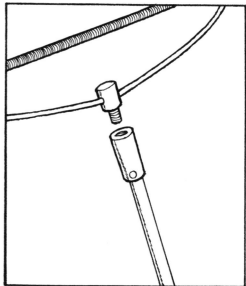

## Float box

This item is invaluable if you want to keep your selection of floats in good condition. The floats are slotted into foam rubber strips, which hold them in place.

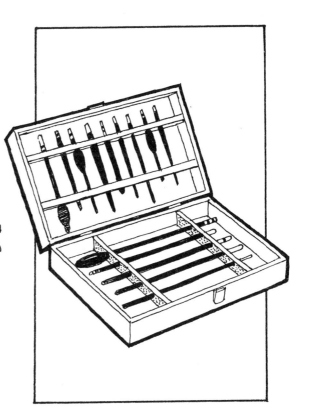

## Bait container

Made from plastic with a snap-on lid. They are available in ½ pint, 1 pint and 2 pint sizes. They are most commonly used for maggots or casters, but can also be used to hold worms, sweetcorn, hemp, and most other baits. When transporting or storing maggots, make sure that the lid is securely fastened.

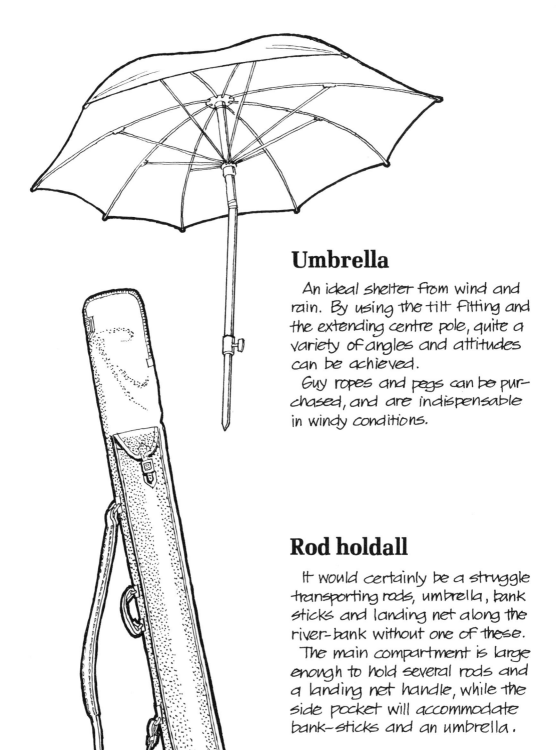

## Umbrella

An ideal shelter from wind and rain. By using the tilt fitting and the extending centre pole, quite a variety of angles and attitudes can be achieved.

Guy ropes and pegs can be purchased, and are indispensable in windy conditions.

## Rod holdall

It would certainly be a struggle transporting rods, umbrella, bank sticks and landing net along the river-bank without one of these.

The main compartment is large enough to hold several rods and a landing net handle, while the side pocket will accommodate bank-sticks and an umbrella.

# Bait dropper

When fishing a fairly deep, fast swim, under the rod tip, this piece of equipment is the answer for presenting loose feed in exactly the right spot. It is attached to the line in the same way as the plummet and lowered into the swim. On making contact with the bottom, the flap opens and loose feed is released into the swim.

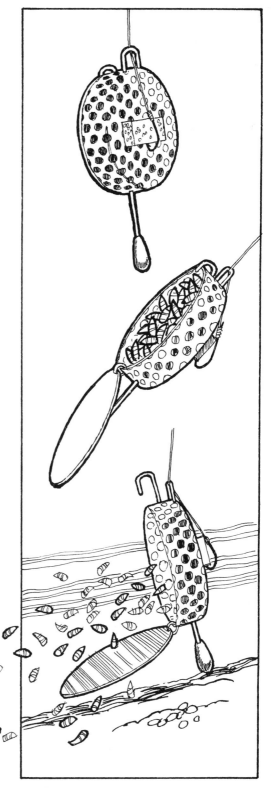

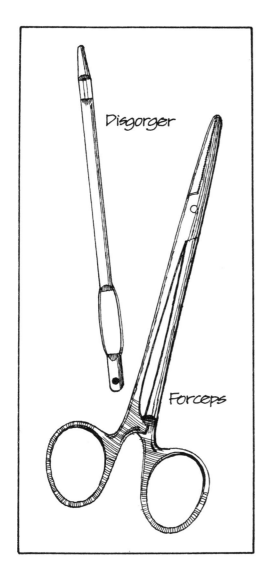

Disgorger

Forceps

## Disgorgers

Artery forceps are more suited to removing large hooks from the bigger species of fish such as carp, tench, chub etc.

The disgorger copes better with smaller hooks on fish like roach or dace.

Disgorgers with sharp points on the end are not recommended.

## Reel case

A reel that is constantly stored loose in the bottom of a tackle container tends to collect bits of grit and dust, which can damage the internal mechanism.

A reel that is stored in a case when not in use is a clean reel, and therefore a more efficient reel.

# Polaroid glasses

These glasses eliminate glare, enabling the angler to see fish beneath the surface of the water.

# Split shot container

Split shot can be purchased in individual plastic containers, or in segmented dispenser-type containers that hold a selection of different size shot. The shot is dispensed via a hole in the lid, which can be rotated to the required position.

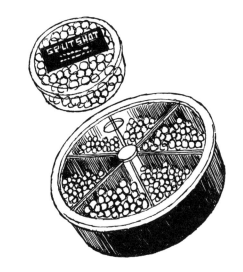

# Spare spools

All fixed-spool reels have spools which are detachable, and easily changed in a matter of seconds. Be prepared for all eventualities by having a collection of spools, each loaded with different breaking strain line.

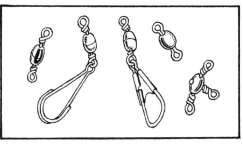

## Swivels

Used for running leger links, and terminal tackle for pike fishing. Some swivels have a link attached (link swivels).

## Float rubbers

Available in a large variety of sizes, either cut to size or in tube form, which allows the angler to tailor his own by cutting through the tube.

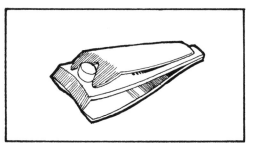

## Nail clippers

The ideal tool for trimming the tag on the end of a knot.

Avon dial scales

Salter spring balance

## Scales

A must for the angler who wants to keep a record of his catches. Weight capacity varies from just a few pounds up to 40lb (18 kg) plus.

# Knots

BLOOD KNOT: For joining two lengths of line of similar thickness. For joining lines of widely differing thickness, the tucked blood knot must be used.

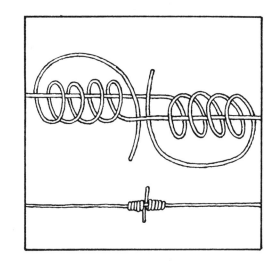

HALF-BLOOD KNOT: For attaching hooks, swivels and leads. This is a practical knot if the wire of the hook, swivel or lead is similar in diameter to the line being used. If the wire is a lot thicker than the line, then a tucked half-blood knot should be used.

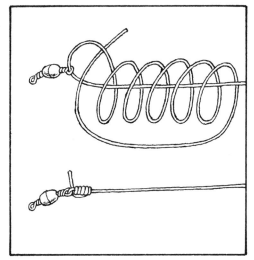

TUCKED HALF-BLOOD KNOT: A more efficient knot than the basic half-blood, and one that should always be employed if large fish are the quarry.

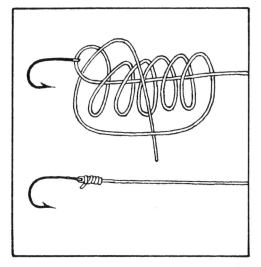

# Knots

TUCKED FULL BLOOD KNOT: For joining line of widely differing thickness. The thinner line must be doubled within the tying area and taken around the thicker line twice as many times.

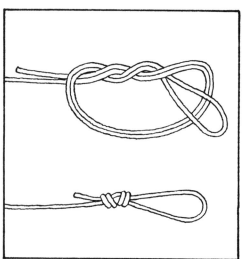

DOUBLE LOOP KNOT: A useful knot for joining a hook length to the main line. A loop is tied to the end of both the hook length and the main line.

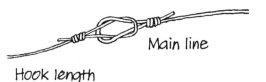

Main line

Hook length

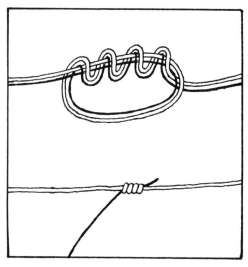

WATER KNOT: An excellent knot for attaching a leader, or a paternoster or leger link.

# Knots

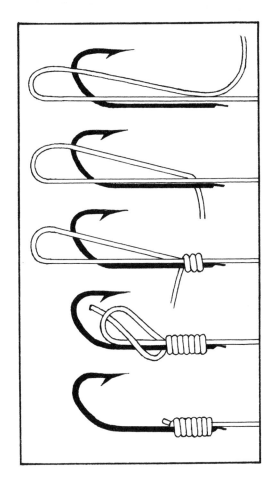

SPADE-END KNOT: Spade-end hooks can be purchased already tied to nylon. However, more and more anglers today are tying their own; shop-bought ones have a nasty habit of coming adrift just at the wrong moment. If you must purchase yours from a tackle shop, check every one of the batch.

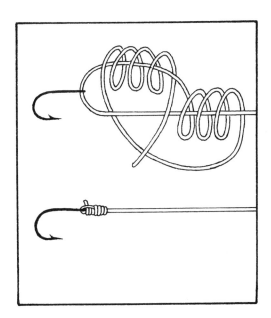

GRINNER KNOT: This knot is equally as good, if not better, than the tucked half blood knot. It just will not come adrift.

Always moisten the line with saliva before tightening any knot. Never jerk the line tight. A firm steady pull is sufficient. Leave about 1/32 in.(1 mm) of tag protruding from the finished knot.